C(

THE SACRAMENTS

EUCHARIST
Bread of Life

Joshua J. Whitfield

Little Rock
Scripture Study

LITURGICAL PRESS
Collegeville, Minnesota

www.littlerockscripture.org

Nihil obstat: Rev. Robert Harren, J.C.L., *Censor Deputatus.*
Imprimatur: ✢ Most Rev. Donald J. Kettler, J.C.L., D.D., Bishop of St. Cloud, December 3, 2020.

Cover design by Ann Blattner. Cover photo: Getty Images.

Photos / illustrations: Pages 8, 11, 15, 16, 20, 22, 25, 26, 31, 37, 40, 42, Getty Images. Used with permission.

ISBN: 978-0-8146-6601-2   978-0-8146-6626-5 (ebook)

Contents

Introduction   4

Prologue   6

The Desert: Covenant and Sacrifice   8

The Synagogue: Food and Drink   20

The City: Discerning the Body   31

Introduction

Alive in the Word brings you resources to deepen your understanding of Scripture, offer meaning for your life today, and help you to pray and act in response to God's word.

Use any volume of **Alive in the Word** in the way best suited to you.

- **For individual learning and reflection,** consider this an invitation to prayerfully journal in response to the questions you find along the way. And be prepared to move from head to heart and then to action.
- **For group learning and reflection,** arrange for three sessions where you will use the material provided as the basis for faith sharing and prayer. You may ask group members to read each chapter in advance and come prepared with questions answered. In this kind of session, plan to be together for about an hour. Or, if your group prefers, read and respond to the questions together without advance preparation. With this approach, it's helpful to plan on spending more time for each group session in order to adequately work through each of the chapters.

- **For a parish-wide event or use within a larger group,** provide each person with a copy of this volume, and allow time during the event for quiet reading, group discussion and prayer, and then a final commitment by each person to some simple action in response to what he or she learned.

This volume on the topic of Eucharist is one of several volumes that explore **Connecting with the Sacraments**. Scripture offers a wealth of ways to reflect on the grace we access in our sacramental lives. By spending time with passages that focus on the spiritual dynamics of each sacrament, our own experiences of the sacraments will deepen. Our ability to appreciate how God works in our lives and in the lives of others will expand.

Prologue

"Blessed are those who have been called to the wedding feast of the Lamb" (Rev 19:9). John of Patmos was commanded to write these words after he heard heaven's victory song, just before he saw a vision of the new Jerusalem, a new heaven and a new earth. An angelic decree, these words declare God's victory and the destiny of the saints. But they are also an invitation at once ancient and new, an invitation still open to each of us.

This book is about the Eucharist. It is about how God repeats this invitation to the "feast" throughout history and how God feeds his people. Scripture is clear: God calls us to be in union with him in a way that is mysterious but very real. Calling the Israelites out of Egypt, calling all people in Christ in the church—what John hears in the book of Revelation is not just an invitation to a feast but an invitation to become a family, to become the people of God. We believe the Eucharist helps to bring this about every day across the world and upon more altars than can be counted, by means of a meal to which Jesus calls us, a meal he has commanded us to repeat.

The three passages we will consider are set respectively in the desert, the synagogue, and the city. Personally fundamental to my own growth in faith, especially faith in the Eucharist, these passages remind me that the Eucharist is essential to Christian life, belonging to every Christian everywhere, and that the Eucharist is part of God's eternal plan. This story that begins in the desert continues in our churches and carries us into heaven, into the very presence of God.

Beyond sharing the Scriptures and my faith with you, what more can I say about this great mystery of the Eucharist? It is beyond words. It is God's mysterious way. But I think it's beautiful. And I hope you do too.

The Desert: Covenant and Sacrifice

Begin with a few quiet moments, asking God to assist you in your prayer and study. Then read this account of a sacred meal from Exodus 24.

Exodus 24:1-11

¹Moses himself was told: Come up to the LORD, you and Aaron, with Nadab, Abihu, and seventy of the elders of Israel. You shall bow down at a distance. ²Moses alone is to come close to the LORD; the others shall not come close, and the people shall not come up with them.

³When Moses came to the people and related all the words and ordinances of the LORD, they all answered with one voice, "We will do everything that the LORD has told us." ⁴Moses then wrote down all the words of the LORD and, rising early in the morning, he built at the foot of the mountain an altar and twelve sacred stones for the twelve tribes of Israel. ⁵Then, having sent young men of the Israelites to offer burnt offerings and sacrifice young bulls as communion offerings to the LORD, ⁶Moses took half of the blood and put it in large bowls; the

other half he splashed on the altar. [7]Taking the book of the covenant, he read it aloud to the people, who answered, "All that the LORD has said, we will hear and do." [8]Then he took the blood and splashed it on the people, saying, "This is the blood of the covenant which the LORD has made with you according to all these words."

[9]Moses then went up with Aaron, Nadab, Abihu, and seventy elders of Israel, [10]and they beheld the God of Israel. Under his feet there appeared to be sapphire tilework, as clear as the sky itself. [11]Yet he did not lay a hand on these chosen Israelites. They saw God, and they ate and drank.

> *Following a brief time of reflection on the desert account from Exodus 24, consider the background information provided below in Setting the Scene. The questions in the margins may be used for personal reflection or group discussion.*

Setting the Scene

In the desert, something remarkable happened. Escaped from Egypt and encamped in the "wilderness of Sinai" (Exod 19:1), former Israelite slaves became the people of God, "a kingdom of priests, a holy nation" (19:6). God cared for them there, feeding and guiding them by miracle and awe along the way. And yet it was excruciatingly difficult. The Israelites grumbled, complained, and sometimes even desired their former subjugation (Exod 17:1-7; Num 11:1-5).

But they learned how to listen. And they even saw God. I've been in that desert. Have you? It's a believable story—that God would cut a covenant and even show himself in so harsh a place. We are vulnerable in the desert. We are not in control; God is.

The first part of Exodus tells of God's liberation of the Hebrews from Egypt, followed by the giving of the Ten Commandments and the covenant at Sinai (Exod 19–23). Exodus 24 describes the solemnization of the covenant in remarkable rituals of ascent, sacrifice, and a meal that is transformed into a mystical, sacred experience that language fails to fully describe.

Here—in covenant, blood, and feast—Moses, his companions, and seventy elders of Israel see God. God is present to them. It is feast. It is communion. For Christians, this extraordinary meal—this remarkable thing that happened in the desert—ultimately points to Jesus and to the sacred meal the church celebrates Sunday by Sunday and every day all over the world.

Scholars have critically debated Exodus 24:1-11 for centuries. It is not difficult to understand why: verses 1 and 2 stand in tension if not contradiction; verses 3-8 seem artificially fitted between verses 1-2 and 9-11; and verse 7 seems to repeat verse 3. We can see why most scholars agree this is a "redacted" text—an edited final product, a fusion of multiple sources.

Yet this shouldn't trouble us. It certainly didn't trouble ancient scholars. Rather than focusing on sources and complex historical background, we'll focus on the passage as it stands—in its final, inspired, canonical form. Thus we will not only receive the story as it is told, but we will also be able to read the details, allusions, and themes within it as elements of a fuller theological and spiritual reading, pointing us ultimately to the Eucharist.

How essential do you think the Eucharist is to the church? How do you understand the relationship between the two?

Exodus 24:1-11 will now be explored a few verses at a time to deepen your understanding of the passage. Reflect on the text and questions along the way.

Understanding the Scene Itself

¹Moses himself was told: Come up to the LORD, you and Aaron, with Nadab, Abihu, and seventy of the elders of Israel. You shall bow down at a distance. ²Moses alone is to come close to the LORD; the others shall not come close, and the people shall not come up with them.

³When Moses came to the people and related all the words and ordinances of the LORD, they all answered with one voice, "We will do everything that the LORD has told us."

The elders went up the mountain only to "bow down." Ascent and prostration seem to be a paradox of worship. Do you ever experience this paradox at Mass or in prayer? How?

God calls Moses and the elders up the mountain. But Moses alone is allowed to "come close to the LORD." The elders and people are to keep various distances. The arrangement is hierarchical: Moses, elders, people. Yet they are all connected. In the elders, all the people of Israel are represented. When the elders voluntarily "bow down" before the Lord, all of Israel, in a sense, bows down with them.

This worship is immediately coupled with obedience. After Moses communicates to the people the "words and ordinances of the LORD"—that is, the Ten Commandments (Exod 20) and subsequent laws (Exod 21–23)—the people reply, "We will do everything that the LORD has told us." The people had declared their obedience earlier in the book of Exodus (19:8) but without hearing the law. Here they are fully informed and so, therefore, is their assent.

"We will do everything that the LORD has told us"! The Israelites quickly failed to keep this promise. Think of all the times you resolved to live a new life and then struggled, failed, succeeded, and failed again. How do you continue in grace?

⁴Moses then wrote down all the words of the LORD and, rising early in the morning, he built at the foot of the mountain an altar and twelve sacred stones for the twelve tribes of Israel. ⁵Then, having sent young men of the Israelites to offer burnt offerings and sacrifice young bulls as communion offerings to the LORD, ⁶Moses took half of the blood and put it in large bowls; the other half he splashed on the altar. ⁷Taking the book of the covenant, he read it aloud to the people, who answered, "All that the LORD has said, we will hear and do." ⁸Then he took the blood and splashed it on the people, saying, "This is the

blood of the covenant which the LORD has made with you according to all these words."

Sacrifice immediately follows. An altar is built at the foot of the mountain, made of twelve pillars representing the twelve tribes of Israel. The altar symbolizes God, and the twelve stones symbolize the foundation of this new "kingdom of priests" (Exod 19:6). This altar will be a place of sacrifice where blood will be shed.

Blood from the sacrifice is "splashed" on both the altar and the people as Moses reads from the book of the covenant. Sacrificial blood signifies several things. First, as blood resulting from death, it is a reminder that sacrifice is a *total* gift of self, not partial. Second, this blood is efficacious. It is powerful and effective. Like other occasions where blood has been shed in the history of Israel, this blood brings about a profound result.

The near-sacrifice of Isaac and the blood of the exodus are exemplary sacrifices in salvation history. Because Abraham did not withhold the very life—the blood—of his son Isaac, his posterity, the promise to Abraham was renewed (Gen 22:16-18). Moses later pointed to this sacrifice, staying God's wrath after the idolatry of the golden calf (Exod 32:13). In Egypt, seeing the blood on the doors of the Israelites, the Lord passed over and kept the "destroyer" away (Exod 12:23). As visceral symbols, each blood sacrifice stands for this: total commitment, even to the point of bloodshed or death. In some instances, blood also pleads for *expiation*—that is, the wiping away of sin (see Lev 4; 16; Heb 9:22).

The image of twelve "sacred stones" calls to mind John's vision of the new Jerusalem and its twelve gates named for Israel's tribes as well as the twelve foundation stones inscribed with the names of the twelve apostles (Rev 21:12-14). How do you understand the connection between Israel, the church, and the heavenly Jerusalem?

This blood of the sacrifice also signifies life and communion. Here blood symbolism is at its most basic. The ancients believed that the life or soul of a body was "in the blood" (Lev 17:11). Across cultures, "blood" also stood for kin. Families share blood. We still understand what "blood brothers" are. Blood signifies a bond of biology or oath, something permanent. This covenant establishes a family, a communion of blood—of life—between God and Israel.

Think of the way blood binds us all, in families and societies. How does blood bind the church?

⁹**Moses then went up with Aaron, Nadab, Abihu, and seventy elders of Israel, ¹⁰and they beheld the God of Israel. Under his feet there appeared to be sapphire tilework, as clear as the sky itself. ¹¹Yet he did not lay a hand on these chosen Israelites. They saw God, and they ate and drank.**

Sacrifice is followed by a sacred meal. This, too, is a binding ritual, a contractual act. Such, for instance, is how Jacob and Laban finally secured their rather tense truce (Gen 31:44-46). Here, however, Israel is bound to God by a covenant (*bĕrîth*), an agreement of promise and responsibility established between parties of infinite inequality.

Elsewhere in the Old Testament, worship and sacred meals also go together. Eating "in the presence of the LORD" was a religious act (Deut 12:7). Isaiah dreamed of an everlasting covenant celebrated in a feast (Isa 55:1-3) and of the mountain of the Lord abundant with "rich food and choice wines" (25:6).

At this feast, however, something rare happens, something difficult to describe. With the elders, Moses ascends again, and there they "behold" God. Language shifts to the metaphorical. Like Ezekiel, they see heaven and "sapphire" (Ezek 1:26). What exactly this means is debated, but it is clearly *theophany*, a manifestation of God. What is remarkable is that Moses and the elders are not struck dead. In a moment of closeness, God shows himself to his covenanted people, and they remain unharmed.

How precisely Moses and the elders "see" God is also debated. The most we can confidently say is that this type of seeing is similar to the kind of vision granted to the prophets who saw God (Num 24:4; Isa 1:1; Amos 1:1). Understanding exactly what happened is not our focus. Rather, what astounds us is the scene as a whole, a scene which strikes the Christian reader as a great prefiguration: after the sacrifice, this small band of Israelites saw God while eating and drinking in the divine presence.

What do you think is meant by Moses and the elders "seeing" God on Sinai? How do you think they "beheld" God? How or when have you seen God?

Jesus' ministry was, in many ways, a ministry of meals. Ever since the wedding at Cana (John 2:1-11), the meals at which Jesus was present always seemed to bear extraordinary significance. They were often messianic signs. The disciples of John, for instance, asked why Jesus' disciples did not fast, and Jesus answered that

the "bridegroom" was with them (Matt 9:14-15; Mark 2:18-22; Luke 5:33-35). When Jesus fed the multitudes, the occasions were understood by those present as messianic signs (Matt 14:13-21; 15:32-39; Mark 6:31-44; 8:1-9; Luke 9:12-17; John 6:1-15). In John's account, the people even tried to make Jesus a king!

Jesus himself spoke of the kingdom of God in terms of a banquet, often a wedding feast (see Matt 22:1-14). Like so many prophets before him, Jesus imagined God's perfect reign in terms of a meal. For Jesus, God's kingdom is like a radically inclusive meal where "the poor and the crippled, the blind and the lame" are the honored guests (Luke 14:21). Essential to Jesus' ministry, the mystical and prophetic idea behind these radical meals was born in the desert. Meals had the potential to be encounters with a God who can "spread a table in the desert" (Ps 78:19; NAB), as was done at Sinai in that ancient covenant meal.

Ultimately, Jesus' ministry of meals was also a ministry of blood. At Jesus' most important meal, the Last Supper, he called his blood the "blood of the covenant" (Matt 26:28; Mark 14:24; or a "new covenant" in Luke 22:20). Here allusion to Exodus 24 is explicit. As at Sinai, blood signifies sacrifice and communion. Now, however, the sacrifice is perfect, and the covenant is "[even] better" (Heb 7:22). In the letter to the Hebrews, Jesus' blood is explicitly related to the blood shed at Sinai. In both sacrifices, a covenant is established and forgiveness is granted (9:11-22). But according to the author of Hebrews, Jesus' sacrifice is more effective because it obtains "eternal redemption" (9:12). Hence, Christ's covenant is "eternal" (13:20); his blood, shed "once for all" (9:12), is still efficacious today.

The Eucharist is for Christians what the rites of Exodus 24:1-11 were for the Israelites at Sinai. Both create the people of God in sacrificial obedience and in blood and life. On Sinai, after sacrifice and meal, Moses and the elders, while eating and drinking, "see" God. Luke's gospel tells a parallel story (24:13-35). After the word of God has been shared, the disciples "see" the risen Christ in the context of a meal. Now theophany is *christophany*; to see God is to see Christ and to recognize him "in the breaking of the bread" (Luke 24:35).

This passage from Exodus marks the beginning of the covenant. What followed was the struggle to live it out faithfully. How is the Eucharist the beginning of the Christian life? Does the Eucharist change your thinking or behavior? How?

Praying the Word / Sacred Reading

Choose a passage from the gospels that you have always associated with the Eucharist. Maybe it is one of the accounts of the Last Supper (Matt 26:26-29; Mark 14:22-25; Luke 22:14-23) or the feeding of the multitudes (Matt 14:13-21; 15:32-39; Mark 6:30-44; 8:1-10; Luke 9:10-17; John 6:1-15), or maybe it is a passage from Acts (2:42-47) or Paul's letters (1 Cor 10:1-22; 11:17-34). Read the passage again prayerfully, but this time meditate upon it within the larger context of Exodus and Sinai, all the way to Revelation and the new Jerusalem. Think about where the passage you have chosen fits within that very big story. And then think about where the Eucharists you have shared in fit within that story. After several moments of reflection, offer this prayer:

Father, you set tables in the wilderness.
In feeding your people, you make them your own.
And in your Son, by his sacrifice and fed with
    his body and blood, we are yours.
May we be obedient to your words, to the way
    you want us to live.
When we fail, may we desire your mercy and
    know your forgiveness.
May we never forget that your covenant is eternal.
And as so many saints have seen you, may we,
    too, see you in the table you set for us
at every Eucharist and in the wildernesses of our
    lives.

Until you come again to invite us to another
    feast, eternal in the kingdom,
we ask this through Christ our Lord. Amen.

Living the Word

*For no special reason, on no special day, prepare
a magnificent meal. Have the family dress up or
invite a few friends. Maybe even throw a small
party. And then, just enjoy it. But notice the smiles
and the laughter; notice how the meal takes on
more than functional significance, how it brings
people together. And then think about what such
a meal would have meant in an earlier time when
food was scarce. Think what it would mean today
in places where food is lacking. Imagine the relief
and pleasure such a meal would offer. And then
think about why God has so often chosen to draw
people to himself in meals and how you can do
the same—in your own home and around your
own table, your own sacred feasts.*

*National
Eucharist
Revival*

The Synagogue: Food and Drink

John 6:51-59

⁵¹"I am the living bread that came down from heaven; whoever eats this bread will live forever; and the bread that I will give is my flesh for the life of the world."

⁵²The Jews quarreled among themselves, saying, "How can this man give us [his] flesh to eat?" ⁵³Jesus said to them, "Amen, amen, I say to you, unless you eat the flesh of the Son of Man and drink his blood, you do not have life within you. ⁵⁴Whoever eats my flesh and drinks my blood has eternal life, and I will raise him on the last day. ⁵⁵For my flesh is true food, and my blood is true drink. ⁵⁶Whoever eats my flesh and drinks my blood remains in me and I in him. ⁵⁷Just as the

living Father sent me and I have life because of the Father, so also the one who feeds on me will have life because of me. [58]This is the bread that came down from heaven. Unlike your ancestors who ate and still died, whoever eats this bread will live forever." [59]These things he said while teaching in the synagogue in Capernaum.

Following a few moments of quiet reflection on Jesus' words, consider the background information provided below in Setting the Scene. Use the questions in the margins for personal reflection or group discussion.

Setting the Scene

Two miracles precede the words Jesus speaks here: the multiplication of the loaves (6:1-15) and his walking on water (6:16-21). I highly recommend reading them—or better yet, all of John 6—before studying this excerpt if possible. These miracles are essential to understanding what follows.

Read John 6

When the messiah came, some believed, so would the manna. This expectation explains the crowd's reaction to the first miracle: they wonder if Jesus is "the Prophet, the one who is to come into the world" (6:14). Jesus feeds them with more bread than they can eat—miraculously and Moses-like—in the wilderness. John calls this miracle a "sign" because it reveals something of who Jesus really is.

The allusions woven into the miracle provoke messianic wonder. Near Passover, Jesus goes "up on the mountain" (6:3) and asks his disciples,

"Where can we buy enough food for them to eat?" (6:5). A young boy with a few fish and loaves of bread provides the stuff for the miracle. Such details echo Exodus, Sinai, Moses, and even Elijah. Even more, this feeding miracle evokes that tense miracle in the desert recorded in Numbers 11. Hungry and tired of manna, the Israelites asked for something more, causing Moses to ask God, "Where can I get meat to give to all this people?" (Num 11:13). Ultimately the people feasted on quail. In Deuteronomy 18:15, Moses promised that God would one day send a "prophet like me." Feeding the multitudes, Jesus is a new Moses; the miracle of Numbers is repeated. Thus the people openly wonder if Jesus is the "Prophet," the promised successor to Moses, the messiah they have hoped for.

Hence the story which immediately follows: a second miracle to interpret the first. Jesus, although Messiah, is not the messiah the people are expecting. Not merely political, not even merely prophetic, *this* messiah walks on water; there is something supernatural about him.

All of this sets up conversation about the miracle of the loaves. Impressed because he fed them and they had their fill, the crowd will now hear Jesus talk about another sort of bread, an even better bread. Earlier he spoke of "water welling up to eternal life" (John 4:14); now he talks of bread that "endures for eternal life" (6:27). He is, as his listeners will learn, speaking of himself, but in a way no one expects.

John 6:22-59 is known as the Bread of Life Discourse. As Jesus delivers this discourse (from which our excerpt is taken), the people resist his words because they don't believe in him. They want a sign. But Jesus insists that faith is required: "I am the bread of life" (6:35). To grasp what Jesus is saying—that in him hunger and thirst are forever satisfied—one must believe that Jesus has been sent by the Father, that he does the will of the Father, and that he grants eternal life to believers, raising them up on the last day (6:36-40).

The crowd begins to murmur like the Israelites grumbled in the desert (6:41; Exod 16:1-16), but they really haven't heard anything yet! At this point, everything Jesus is saying can be understood within Jewish eschatological hope and the Wisdom tradition. Hearing him talk, one could simply think Jesus is claiming to be Wisdom or the messiah ushering in the final victorious banquet of God (see Prov 9; Isa 55:1-3; 65:11-13).

Jesus doesn't argue with the crowd. He just says, "Stop murmuring" (6:43). Faith is faith. "Everyone who listens to my Father and learns from him comes to me" (6:45). Such is the blunt mystery of it, the simple inscrutable gift of faith. And so, Jesus simply proclaims truth: whoever believes has eternal life. Jesus is the Bread of Life. The ancient manna did not save; the new manna from heaven will. Such is how Jesus

In the famous hymn *Adoro te devote,* St. Thomas Aquinas wrote: "I believe whatever the Son of God has said." From your reading of John 6, what does faith in Christ have to do with belief in the Eucharist?

answers their grumbling, with a straightforward proclamation demanding faith. And for what Jesus will say next (vv. 51-59), they'll need it!

John 6:51-59 will now be explored a few verses at a time. The commentary will help you deepen your understanding of the passage, and the questions in the margins will aid you in reflection and discussion

Understanding the Scene Itself

[51]"I am the living bread that came down from heaven; whoever eats this bread will live forever; and the bread that I will give is my flesh for the life of the world."

Jesus calling himself "bread" implies a purpose: to feed. The giver of "living water" (John 4:10) is also the "living bread" whose goal is to eliminate hunger and thirst (6:35). This is why Jesus gives his "flesh for the life of the world." The verb "to give" here recalls at least two related things: the sacrifice of the cross and the Last Supper. Jesus told Nicodemus, "God so loved the world that he gave his only Son" (3:16), and at the Last Supper, Jesus identifies his body in bread and says it is "given for you" (Luke 22:19; see also Matt 26:26; Mark 14:22). Jesus is showing us that in the miracles of feeding, as well as on the cross and in the Eucharist, this "living bread" is blessed, broken, and given (see John 6:11; Matt 14:14; 15:36; Mark 6:42; 8:6; Luke 9:16).

This "living bread" is Jesus' "flesh." The use of the Greek word *sarx* ("flesh") recalls the central mystery described in the prologue of John's gospel: the declaration that the "Word became flesh" (1:14). This mystery of the incarnation—the truth that Jesus Christ has "come in the flesh" (1 John 4:2)—is the foundation of all other mysteries of our faith.

For Jesus to speak of his flesh here is to state, simply and starkly, that the "living bread" he speaks of is genuinely his body. It is as if Jesus is emphatically saying, "It's me!" No longer is Jesus speaking merely in ancient idioms. He is revealing something new: God in the flesh—sacrificed, risen, and shared—becomes living bread.

How does Jesus' flesh given "for the life of the world" relate to the Last Supper and the cross?

⁵²The Jews quarreled among themselves, saying, "How can this man give us [his] flesh to eat?" ⁵³Jesus said to them, "Amen, amen, I say to you, unless you eat the flesh of the Son of Man and drink his blood, you do not have life within you.

The grumbling of the crowd only gets worse. To those present, it is absurd and even grotesque to think that "this man" can offer his flesh to eat, no matter what wonders he has done! The crowd's questioning is intense and aggressive. Behind their grumbling is the ancient horror of cannibalism and drinking blood (see Gen 9:4; Zech 11:9). Looking upon Jesus without faith, seeing him as only a man, the people cannot help but misunderstand his words.

Note that Jesus speaks here for the first time of his blood, emphasizing that it is his real and entire self that satisfies hunger and thirst (6:35). But there is a deeper meaning here as well. As we discussed in the previous chapter, life is in blood (Lev 17:11), so to drink the blood of Jesus is to have his "life within you" (6:53).

⁵⁴Whoever eats my flesh and drinks my blood has eternal life, and I will raise him on the last day. ⁵⁵For my flesh is true food, and my blood is true drink. ⁵⁶Whoever eats my flesh and drinks my blood remains in me and I in him.

Notice again that Jesus doesn't argue. He simply declares. One must eat the flesh and drink the blood of the Son of Man not only to have *life* but to have *eternal life*. What distinction is Jesus making here? Perhaps he is suggesting that the life he gives is lived so "abundantly" (John 10:10) that it becomes eternal. Whatever the case, Jesus' flesh is a pledge of the new life to be lived in the kingdom to come (Mark 14:25; Luke 22:18; 1 Cor 11:26).

This bread, his flesh, bestows eternal life because it "endures for eternal life" (6:27) and because, by eating it, one "remains" in the Son, who also remains in the Father. The verb that is translated "endures" in verse 27 and "re-

How does Jesus answer—or not answer—those who "murmured" at his teaching? What can we learn from Jesus' approach to those who disagree with him?

mains" in verse 56 is the same word in Greek—
menein—and in John's gospel, it does a lot of
theological work. Most importantly, *menein*
describes how the Father, the Son, and the Spirit
"remain" in each other and how the disciples
of Jesus "remain" in him. The night before his
death, Jesus says to his disciples, "Remain in
me, as I remain in you" (15:4). He insists that
his "flesh is true food" and his "blood is true
drink" (6:55). Jesus is not being gentle with his
murmuring listeners! In fact, he's almost being
crude. The word translated as "eat" (*trōgein*) in
verse 56 is better understood as "chew." Jesus
makes shockingly clear that he is doing much
more than borrowing the ideas and language of
the Wisdom tradition. He's talking about something literally edible.

Jesus insists upon faith, but he does not explain the Bread of Life. Later theologians will
articulate the church's theology of transubstan-
tiation, a theology with its own history that is
beyond the scope of this commentary. At this
point, it is enough to say that we can understand
Jesus to be talking about what we now call "real
presence": his body and blood present in bread
and wine. This primitive biblical faith is sum-
marized by the *Catechism of the Catholic
Church* in its clear statement that in the Eucharist, "Christ is thus really and mysteriously made
present" (1357).

This is all one needs to begin: simple faith in
the Son on whom the Father "set his seal" (6:27)
and faith that the bread and wine he gives is
what he declares it to be—himself as true food.

Early Christians were often accused of cannibalism due to their eucharistic celebrations. It seems there were similar concerns in Capernaum. How would you explain why eating and drinking the body and blood of Jesus is not cannibalism?

Jesus insists that his body is "true food" and his blood is "true drink." How do Jesus' words indicate that this is more than mere symbolism? How might you have responded to Jesus' graphic words?

[57]Just as the living Father sent me and I have life because of the Father, so also the one who feeds on me will have life because of me. [58]This is the bread that came down from heaven. Unlike your ancestors who ate and still died, whoever eats this bread will live forever." [59]These things he said while teaching in the synagogue in Capernaum.

In mood and tone, Jesus' interaction with those in Capernaum is like God's interaction with the Israelites when they grumbled for manna and meat (Exod 16:1-15; Num 11:1-35): "I have heard the grumbling of the Israelites. Tell them: In the evening twilight you will eat meat, and in the morning you will have your fill of bread, and then you will know that I, the LORD, am your God" (Exod 16:12). Jesus speaks in the synagogue in Capernaum with the same tone, the same desert urgency, like God leading his people from slavery into the Promised Land once again.

This connection between Jesus and the Father spills over into the life of Jesus' disciples: by remaining in Jesus, the disciples remain in the Father. This is what the *Catechism of the Catholic Church* calls the "sacramental economy" (1076). This is how God uses sacraments to unite believers to him: by feeding them with bread and wine, which is really yet mysteriously the body and blood of the Son, who remains in both the Spirit and the Father. As Pope St. John Paul II explained, this is how in the Eucharist we are "immersed in the ineffable unity of the three divine Persons" (*Ecclesia de Eucharistia*, 50). By the gift of faith and living bread, we become, sacramentally, sharers in the divine nature (2 Pet 1:4).

The rest of the chapter won't surprise us. Most of Jesus' listeners, if not all but the Twelve, leave him. To the Twelve, Jesus simply says, "Does this shock you?" (6:61) and then, "Do you also want to leave?" (6:67). This last question provokes Peter's faith: "Master, to whom shall we go? You have the words of eternal life. We have come to believe and are convinced that you are the Holy One of God" (6:68-69). This is the faith demanded of every Christian.

> Why do you think there is widespread disbelief in the real presence of Jesus in the Eucharist? How would you help someone struggling with Catholic faith in the Eucharist?

Master, to whom shall we go? You have the words of eternal life.
John 6:68

Unconditionally

Praying the Word / Sacred Reading

Father of the Bread of Life,
· thank you for sending your Son into the world,
for giving him to us so that we may believe in
   him for eternal life.
Thank you, Living Bread,
for giving your flesh for the life of the world—
   on the cross and on the altar.

We offer you thanks that you give us your true
    body and true blood,
that you desire us so much that you give us your
    very self.
And thank you, Holy Spirit,
remaining with the Father and the Son.
By you and in you, we too remain
in the Blessed Trinity by faith and word and
    sacrament.
Holy and undivided Trinity,
we praise you.
Remain with us, your church, and increase our
    faith,
that you may lead us, your pilgrim, wandering
    people
still seeking tables in the wilderness,
until we reach your Promised Land.
Amen.

Living the Word

*Spend time before the Blessed Sacrament, quiet
and alone before the tabernacle. Read John 6 in
the presence of the Lord in the Eucharist. But first,
pray to Jesus that he might open your mind and
heart, giving you even greater faith and understanding. Read Jesus' words in John 6, consciously
aware that you are in the presence of the one who
spoke them. And then give thanks to be so close
to God, to the flesh he still gives for the life of the
world—which includes you. Be silent for a while,
simply present to the one who is present to you,
and savor it. Ask him to speak to you. Then listen.*

The City: Discerning the Body

Begin in quiet reflection as you ask God to be with you in your prayer and study. Then read this instructive passage about Eucharist and community that Paul wrote to the young church in Corinth.

1 Corinthians 11:23-29

[23]For I received from the Lord what I also handed on to you, that the Lord Jesus, on the night he was handed over, took bread, [24]and, after he had given thanks, broke it and said, "This is my body that is for you. Do this in remembrance of me." [25]In the same way also the cup, after supper, saying, "This cup is the new covenant in my blood. Do this, as often as you drink it, in remembrance of me." [26]For as often as you eat this bread and drink the cup, you proclaim the death of the Lord until he comes.

²⁷Therefore whoever eats the bread or drinks the cup of the Lord unworthily will have to answer for the body and blood of the Lord. ²⁸A person should examine himself, and so eat the bread and drink the cup. ²⁹For anyone who eats and drinks without discerning the body, eats and drinks judgment on himself.

Following a few moments of quiet reflection, consider the background information provided below in Setting the Scene. Continue using the questions in the margins for personal reflection or group discussion.

Setting the Scene

Corinth was an ancient city, destroyed by the Romans but reestablished by Julius Caesar in 44 BCE. By the time Paul arrived a little more than a century later, it was a diverse, booming, commercial city, home to both Greeks and Romans. Also religiously diverse—as Paul wrote, full of "many 'gods' and many 'lords' "—Corinth boasted numerous pagan cults, as well as a sizeable Jewish population (1 Cor 8:5).

The Christians of Corinth were diverse too. They were rich, middle class, poor, slaves, and former slaves. Most were Gentiles; fewer were Jews. All were one in Christ, of course, yet given their diversity and the fact that they were, as Paul said, still "infants" in faith (1 Cor 3:1), differences and disagreements were bound to arise among them. There were also inevitable misunderstandings about how exactly they should live out their faith, about the changes believing in

Christ demanded of their lives. What of their old way of life could remain the same? What must change? These were difficult questions.

After hearing from several people about what was going on in Corinth (1 Cor 1:11; 16:17), Paul worried the Corinthians were not coming up with the right answers. Sexual immorality, drunkenness, and factionalism all marked the community. Some members of the community were tribalizing their opinions—claiming loyalty to Paul, or Apollos, or Cephas (1 Cor 1:12). For Paul, this factionalism undermined the very nature of the church. The Christian community is Christ's presence, the Body of Christ active in the world. It is "called to be holy" or set apart (1 Cor 1:2). Believers are *adelphoi*, brothers and sisters living together, living differently from others in the world. Paul exhorted the divided Corinthians to grow in unity, urging "that there be no divisions among you, but that you be united in the same mind and in the same purpose" (1 Cor 1:10). This call to unity and harmony was a truth the Corinthians urgently needed to apply to their celebration of the Eucharist.

The verses we will examine here are the New Testament's earliest account of the Lord's Supper, written well before the gospels. Here Paul is rehearsing very early tradition, echoing the most primary elements of Christian experience. His purpose is to call the Corinthians back to a more authentic eucharistic practice and toward a more thoroughly eucharistic way of life.

Before examining this excerpt in detail, it is necessary to understand why Paul invokes this tradition. What were the problems Paul saw with the way the Corinthians celebrated and lived out the Eucharist?

First, Paul addresses the issue of the sanctity of the community. In 1 Corinthians 10, we read Paul's exhortation to eucharistic holiness. Paul is reminding the Corinthians that to be "sanctified in Christ Jesus" (1 Cor 1:2) is about more than moral purity; it also means they must not participate in any other form of worship. Paul offers a warning: just as the Israelites in the desert were, in a sense, "baptized" and nourished with spiritual food and drink yet still died, so too might the Corinthians perish, even though they have also been baptized and spiritually fed, if they participate in pagan worship (1 Cor 10:1-4). Sharing in the bread and wine of the Eucharist is "a participation" in the very body and blood of Christ (1 Cor 10:16-17). The Greek word for "participation" is *koinonia*, implying a deeper-than-ordinary bond, a spiritual and religious communion founded upon Christ's sacrifice, which is exclusive. Paul's warning is clear: "You cannot partake of the table of the Lord and of the table of demons" (1 Cor 10:21). Holiness implies religious exclusivity.

Paul's other concern was unity, which he turns to in 1 Corinthians 11. Indeed, the way the Corinthians celebrated the Eucharist troubled Paul deeply, so much that he wondered if the shared meal could be called the Lord's Supper at all (1 Cor 11:20). When the Corinthians came to-

How is your community holy? How does your community live in unity? What does the Eucharist have to do with it?

Common
Belief

anchor

Remembrance

gether to worship, they did not come together in a manner reflecting their unity in Christ. Rather, social divisions remained apparent and were even accentuated by how they worshiped. Although we do not know exactly how the Eucharist was celebrated in Corinth or at what point in the fellowship (*agape*) meal the sharing of the body and blood of Christ fit in, it is clear that when they came together for the Lord's Supper, they failed to wait for one another (11:33). Wealthier members of the community, at more leisure, ate before poorer members arrived after a day's work. Also, if these meals were potluck as was common in Hellenistic culture, richer members would enjoy better food and more of it. If the fare was provided, it is likely that those nearer and dearest to the host—that is, the rich—ate better than those who were not—that is, the poor. On top of this, some were even getting drunk while others went hungry (11:21). This is why Paul bluntly said, "I do not praise you," and accused them of "contempt for the church of God" (11:22).

Why is it essential that we embrace the social dimension of the Eucharist rather than only experiencing it individualistically? How would you explain the balance?

The way the Corinthian Christians came together for fellowship and Eucharist highlighted divisions rather than erased them, especially between rich and poor. Instead of allowing the Eucharist to transform social divisions, they allowed social divisions to deform the Eucharist. In the end, Paul said this practice did "more harm than good" (11:17). It contradicted the unity they had in Christ.

1 Corinthians 11:23-29 will now be explored a few verses at a time to deepen your understanding of the passage. Spend time with the text and the questions along the way.

Understanding the Scene Itself

23For I received from the Lord what I also handed on to you . . .

Like a rabbi offering *halakah*, Paul intends to correct Corinthian error. *Halakah*, from the verb "to walk," refers to Jewish law developed and handed on over the centuries. This is the origin of the Christian concept of tradition. *Paradosis* (Greek for "tradition") means "to hand over." Here Paul is "handing over" to the Corinthians a eucharistic tradition that he hopes will remind them how to walk the eucharistic walk.

The tradition Paul evokes is "from the Lord." This is not necessarily a claim of personal revelation; rather, Paul is saying that what he is handing on ultimately comes from Jesus. This is not the "tradition of the elders" (Mark 7:5) but the tradition of Jesus Christ. Paul is returning to the central source, the beginning of the eucharistic mystery itself.

23. . . that the Lord Jesus, on the night he was handed over, took bread, 24and, after he had given thanks, broke it and said, "This is my body that is for you. Do this in remembrance of me." 25In the same way also the cup, after supper, saying, "This cup is the new covenant in my

blood. Do this, as often as you drink it, in remembrance of me."

Paul relates what must have been common tradition in the very early Christian community. The language he uses is also found in the gospels: "took bread," "given thanks," "broke it," "this is my body," and references to "covenant" are found not only in gospel accounts of the Lord's Supper, but some elements are also present in the Emmaus story (Luke 24:30) as well as accounts of the feeding of the multitudes (Matt 14:19; 15:36; Mark 6:41; 8:6; Luke 9:16; John 6:11). Paul's rehearsal of the tradition is closest to Luke's (22:14-20). The parallelism found in these verses ("This is my body/Do this" and "This cup/Do this") suggests this tradition is liturgical.

Paul shares what the Lord did "the night he was handed over" (1 Cor 11:23). What Jesus did, of course, belongs to the larger story of God feeding his people, from the desert to the new Jerusalem. It belongs to that of which the psalmist sang, the table and the overflowing cup provided in the valley of the shadow of death, even in the presence of enemies (Ps 23:4-5). God in Christ, surrounded by enemies the night before his death, feeds the disciples.

What is unique, though, is that this food is flesh and this wine is blood. Paul simply repeats the words—"This is my body" and "This cup is the new covenant in my blood"—without theological interpretation, yet with understated realism. This is the personal gift of Christ himself in his body and blood; he himself is food and drink.

Not to be overlooked are the sacrifices that give this ritual meaning. The body Jesus offers is "for you" (11:24). The cup is "the new covenant in my blood" (11:25). Such language evokes cultic sacrifice, recalling the covenant ratified in the desert in sacrificial blood and the meal turned mystical on the mountain (Exod 24:1-11). The description of this covenant as "new" evokes Jeremiah's prophecy of a new covenant—a covenant by which sin is forgiven and through which the law is written upon hearts and all "from least to greatest" know the Lord (Jer 31:31-34). Jesus fulfills Jeremiah's hope. The Eucharist *is* the new covenant.

Included in the phrase "for you" are disciples both past and present. Not merely recounting a historical moment, the reason Paul rehearses the eucharistic tradition is because this new covenant in Christ's body and blood is still in effect. Such is the implication of the twice-repeated command: "Do this in remembrance of me" (11:24-25). To remember in the biblical sense

Reflect on how this challenging, transforming role of the Eucharist is a sign of the true presence of Christ in the Eucharist. How does Jesus Christ, present in the Eucharist, transform you?

"DO THIS IN REMEMBRANCE OF ME."
1 COR 11:24

involves more than mental recall. Rather, to remember is to call forth present action. Similar to a spouse remembering his or her wedding vows or a parent saying to a child, "Remember, I said to clean your room," when "remembrance" is invoked in Scripture, its purpose is to make what is remembered present and real. The Greek term is *anamnesis*, and it implies bringing historical moments into the present, especially moments involving God. Thus the command "Do this in remembrance of me" establishes a connection between the first Lord's Supper in the Upper Room and all those Suppers celebrated in Corinth. This timeless bond is made possible by the divine presence. It is real because Jesus is the Lord, "the same yesterday, today, and forever" (Heb 13:8).

²⁶For as often as you eat this bread and drink the cup, you proclaim the death of the Lord until he comes.

To make Jesus present is also to make his death present. More precisely, when Jesus is made present in the Eucharist, his death is announced. This is a proclamation that will last until Christ returns in glory. His person and his passion cannot be separated. Here Paul locates the Corinthians' celebration of the Eucharist within eschatological time. That is, not only is the Eucharist they celebrate connected to the way God fed his people throughout history and now in Christ, but it is also related to the Second Coming. Jesus is the "Lord" for whom Christians pray "*Marana tha*" (Aramaic for "Come, Lord"; 1 Cor 16:22). By situating the Eucharist thus within God's cosmic timing, Paul underlines the purpose of the Eucharist: to make real the dynamic presence of Jesus and, necessarily, the death of Jesus, until he returns.

This emphasis on the Eucharist as an ongoing proclamation of the death of Jesus helps us understand why Paul retells the tradition of the Lord's Supper in the first place. If the Eucharist announces the "death of the Lord," then that is precisely what the Corinthian gatherings were *not* doing. Jesus' death and resurrection "reconcile all things," bringing together by the blood of Christ those "who once were far off" from each other (Col 1:20; Eph 2:11-22). To proclaim the death of the risen Lord

is to proclaim its reconciling power; it is to proclaim the gathering together of disparate peoples.

But in Corinth, each person was eating his or her own meal (1 Cor 11:21). They were not waiting for one another (11:33). Social divisions, instead of being erased by the Eucharist, were blatantly pronounced. This is why Paul dared to suggest that what the Corinthians were doing was not the Lord's Supper. It did not proclaim what the Eucharist proclaims: the unifying power of the death of Jesus Christ.

[27]Therefore whoever eats the bread or drinks the cup of the Lord unworthily will have to answer for the body and blood of the Lord. [28]A person should examine himself, and so eat the bread and drink the cup. [29]For anyone who eats and drinks without discerning the body, eats and drinks judgment on himself.

To this fractured community, Paul now writes of judgment. To encounter Christ is to encounter judgment—it is either to be saved by faith or condemned in disbelief (John 3:18; 5:24). To encounter Christ in the Eucharist is to encounter the same judgment. According to Paul, the Eucharist is an instrument of the Lord's judgment. Celebrated between the Upper Room and the Second Coming, the Eucharist anticipates the latter, calling Christians to practice self-examination in the interval, judging themselves according to the holiness and unity of Christ.

Thinking of the Eucharist the way Paul asked the Corinthians to think about it, do you feel called to change anything about the way you participate in Mass? How might your community celebrate Mass with a new emphasis or understanding?

Have you ever considered the Eucharist to be an instrument of judgment? How might the Eucharist "discipline" the community as a challenging, transforming instrument of change?

This is what Paul means by "discerning the body" (1 Cor 11:29). If Christ is present in the Eucharist, and if the church is the Body of Christ, then the unity which is Christ must be visible in his Body, the church. Here Paul cuts to the heart of the problem of the Eucharist as celebrated in Corinth, where each was eating "his own supper," thereby showing "contempt for the church of God" (11:21-22). Such disunity proved the Corinthians had failed to examine themselves and "discern the body," which is why they were in danger.

Are there broader ethical implications to the Eucharist? What responsibility do believers bear for one another as members of the eucharistic community?

In the city, as in the desert and the synagogue, God desired to feed his people. Now God's people were of all kinds and from all walks of life—all different but of one faith. This is why the Corinthians needed to wait for one another: God wanted to feed them all.

Praying the Word / Sacred Reading

Come, Lord Jesus, into my community;
enter, too, my heart.
Present in the Eucharist,
we are made your Body, the church.
May we be what you make us:
the kingdom, the sheepfold,
the temple, the dwelling place of God in the Spirit.
Make us proclaimers of your death:
by holiness and unity,
by single-minded devotion to you, Lord Jesus,
and to each other,
especially the least among us.
And finally, Lord, inspire in me
and in my brothers and sisters
a longing for your return,
that praying in truth *"Marana tha!"*
we may greet you,
the Lord of all our Eucharists.
Amen.

Living the Word

*Meditate upon one of the Eucharistic Prayers of
the church, savoring each word and phrase. (You
can find the Eucharistic Prayers in a missal or
by searching online.) In your prayerful reading,
understand what the church is praying. Notice
how the church is envisioned socially: a body
including the pope, bishops, believers throughout the world—all peoples. And then reflect
upon your community—on those you know and
those you don't. Ask God to show you how to*

draw closer to your community: in service, in simple affection, in meeting someone new, in forgiveness. Ask God to show you what it means to proclaim the death of the Lord Jesus in your community. And then pray for the stirring of the Holy Spirit, for the resolve to take the first step. And then go: build up the Body of Christ!